Original title:

Breeze Over the Island

Copyright © 2025 Creative Arts Management OÜ
All rights reserved.

Author: Elliot Harrison
ISBN HARDBACK: 978-1-80581-571-6
ISBN PAPERBACK: 978-1-80581-098-8
ISBN EBOOK: 978-1-80581-571-6

The Golden Glow of Dusk's Arrival

The sun dips low, a golden ray,
A crab runs by, in a funny sway.
Flip-flops flop with a joyful sound,
While seagulls dive, all around.

Laughter echoes, the sand so warm,
A turtle's dance becomes the norm.
Children giggle, chasing a kite,
As the day fades into night.

A parrot squawks, oh what a fuss,
Dressed in style, just like us!
Palm trees swaying, doing their jig,
In the shade, we dance a big wig.

As lanterns flicker, shadows play,
A fish jumps high, making our day.
With all this joy, oh who would guess,
Dusk's glow brings such silliness!

Unveiling the Island's Quiet Beauty

The coconuts roll with a bouncy cheer,
One hits a crab, oh dear, oh dear!
The waves come in with a splashy greet,
Seagulls hover for a tasty treat.

A hammock sways, a nap in sight,
But a squirrel's antics give a fright.
He dances near, steals a chip,
Leaving us laughing, we can't help but flip.

The sunset paints with colors so bold,
While jellyfish jiggle, stories unfold.
A lazy dog snoozes, tail a-wag,
While we sip on drinks and wave our flag.

Beneath the stars, the island glows,
Whispers of laughter, humor flows.
With every giggle, we find delight,
In the night air, everything feels right.

Wings of Seagulls and Salted Air

The seagulls squawk, they dive and dance,
Their antics make me take a chance.
I wave my arms, they tilt and glide,
Must think I'm weird, but still I tried.

With salty kisses on my face,
These feathery friends are in the race.
They steal my chips with daring flair,
And I just laugh, without a care.

The Painting of a Perfect Day

Paint splatters on the sky so blue,
A child tosses sand, quite a view.
I try to catch it, what a fail,
Instead, I'm a walking sand trail!

Umbrellas fly like kites in flight,
My drink is now a sandy sight.
But laughter floats on every wave,
A masterpiece, I must be brave.

Whirlwinds of Laughter

A coconut falls right on my head,
I laugh so hard, almost misread.
My picnic's ruined by a cheeky crow,
It snatches my sandwich, off it goes!

The tides pull me in like a playful friend,
I chase my hat, oh when will it end?
But joy erupts in every splash,
I'm soaking wet but what a laugh!

Lost in the Island's Warm Embrace

In flip-flops I trudge through thick sand,
A crab scuttles by, oh so grand!
I wave hello, it gives a stare,
Who knew a pinch would be so rare?

My towel's a sail, I might just drift,
But my sunblock's misplaced, what a gift!
The sun sets down, we share a cheer,
With goofy smiles, it's the best time here.

The Touch of Sunlit Horizons

The parrot squawks with glee,
Chasing away my morning tea.
With every flap, it steals my snack,
A feathery thief, I can't keep track.

The sunbeams dance on sandy feet,
While tourists trip on their own seat.
I wave to dolphins, they laugh with me,
In this island life, we're all carefree.

Chasing Shadows in Warm Aeolian Currents

The shadows play beneath the palms,
Jumping jacks and silly calms.
A crab walks sideways, full of pride,
While I'm tripping, I can hardly hide.

Giggles rise on the salty air,
As children chase a seagull rare.
It swoops for chips, but what a brawl,
As everyone screams, 'That's mine, not all!'

Gentle Spirits of the Shoreline

The waves whisper jokes to the shore,
While shells giggle, 'Tell us more!'
A jellyfish does a wobbly jig,
While I try to catch it, feeling big.

The sun lies low, a golden grin,
And crabs applaud my awkward spin.
But a wave rolls in with a cheeky splash,
And my dance ends in a soggy crash!

Gazing into Horizon's Heart

I gaze afar with wide-eyed glee,
See a boat bobbing, but not me!
With seagulls laughing, I wave my arms,
Hoping to catch their wave of charms.

The sun is setting, a vibrant fuss,
While sandcastles lean, scheming to discuss.
With hats askew and laughter loud,
We toast to mishaps, feeling proud!

Twilight Whispers Beneath Starry Canopies

In the evening glow, we giggle loud,
A firefly's dance draws quite the crowd.
The stars above twinkle and tease,
While the crickets chirp in perfect keys.

We spot a crab wearing a hat,
And wonder how it got so fat.
Laughter bursts, a comet's flight,
In the night, everything feels right.

Wandering Musings by the Water's Edge

Footprints in sand, a clumsy trace,
Trying to keep up with the waves' embrace.
A splash on my leg, oh what a scene,
The fish just winked, or so I mean.

Seagulls squawk in a pouffy parade,
Fumbling their landings, quite unafraid.
With shells as our treasures, we'll giggle and tread,
As the tide keeps crashing, it won't let us head!

The Veil of Tranquil Moments

In sloshing shoes, we dance and sway,
While the sand joins in, making clay.
A hermit crab takes one look and scoffs,
As we waltz along, shaking off our scoffs.

Bamboo drinks bearing fruit that spins,
Chasing our thoughts like whimsical winds.
Each moment captured is a funny joke,
Wrapped in a blanket of giggles and smoke.

Petals Dancing on Ocean Breezes

Flowers tumble like they lost a bet,
Playing tag with the jellyfish set.
A playful splash plus a daring spin,
Leaves us grinning, with hearts so thin.

We chase the petals, colorful fate,
While lost in laughter, we contemplate.
Oh, what a mess, yet pure delight,
As the petals twirl into the night.

Tides of Tranquility

Seagulls squawk, a noisy crew,
They steal my chips, oh how they flew!
Sandy toes and salty hair,
Anyone seen my floppy chair?

The sun does shine, yet I am pale,
A lobster red, I tell the tale!
Shells roll in like tiny cars,
Claiming the beach, stealing stars.

Echoes of a Summer's Hug

Fried shrimp dance on my plate with glee,
I wave my hands, but they won't flee.
Chasing waves, I trip like a fool,
Digging a hole, that's my new school!

Ice cream drips, a messy affair,
Sunshine giggles, I've lost my flair.
With laughter ringing, we all do play,
Counting seagulls on this fine day.

Swaying Palms and Open Skies

Palm trees sway in a comical dance,
Dancing with shadows, given a chance.
Cool drinks spill on my favorite shirt,
A sticky mess, oh how it hurts!

The ocean laughs, it tickles my toes,
As I slip softly, everyone knows.
The waves crash loud, but I don't care,
Just part of the fun, as I splash everywhere!

Lullabies of the Serene Sea

Coconuts fall with a thud from above,
I dodge and weave, in jest I shove.
A crab scuttles, giving me a stare,
"Why so serious?" it seems to declare!

Flip-flops flinging, they fly through the air,
A laugh escapes, my troubles are rare.
As the sun dips low, we gather near,
Sharing jokes, with a glass of cheer!

Lurking Dolphins in a Gentle Flow

With flip and splash, they tease the waves,
Dolphins giggle, doing the braves.
They peek and dive, a playful sight,
Making the tourists laugh in delight.

With swirls and spins, they plot their fun,
Stealing snacks from the beach-goers run.
A splashy heist, what a sight to see,
These clever fish, oh they're so free!

Celestial Dance of the Caribbean Air

The sun dips low, it's quite a show,
Seagulls groove in a synchronized flow.
Clouds wobble in the twilight gleam,
Nature's comedy, a marvelous dream.

Palm trees sway with an awkward twist,
Who knew they had moves on a blissful list?
Crickets chirp, joining in the song,
Making the night feel silly and strong.

A Voyage on the Wind's Canvas

Kites soar high, caught in the air,
Like offbeat dancers with tousled hair.
They giggle and twirl, such a sight to behold,
On a sea of laughter, stories unfold.

Mischief abounds with the wind's sweet grace,
It tickles the cheeks, makes a funny face.
Sailing along on cushions of cheer,
Who knew the sky could be so dear?

Serenity at the Water's Fringe

The tide rolls in with a frothy cheer,
Tickling toes and whispering near.
Children chase waves with squeals of delight,
Chasing the foamy tips into the night.

Shells are treasures, but which one to pick?
A game of fun, it goes on quite thick.
The sand's a canvas, creations abound,
Where silly smiles and joy are found.

The Laughter of the Wind

A tickling gust flies by,
It whispers jokes to trees,
The palm fronds giggle loud,
As coconuts roll with ease.

Seagulls caw their witty quips,
While crabs wear goofy hats,
The ocean waves chuckle soft,
As dolphins dance in spats.

Flip-flops flap on sandy toes,
As if they're having fun,
A hula hoop of laughter,
Underneath a glowing sun.

So join the mirthful chorus,
Of nature's playful ways,
Where every mighty gust of wind,
Turns frowns to sunny days.

Porcelain Dreams of Tidal Love

Crabs in tuxedos, dancing crabs,
Frolicking beneath the moon,
They spin and twirl on porcelain sands,
With a rhythm all their own.

Starfish serenade the waves,
With voices deep and sly,
While oysters crack their silly jokes,
As the tide goes rolling by.

Seashells whisper secrets sweet,
In echoes soft and fine,
Each grain of sand has grinned so wide,
Love's humor in design.

Underneath the starlit sky,
Where laughter floats like doves,
The tidal pull, a playful tease,
In porcelain dreams of loves.

Echoes of a Summer's Embrace

A sunbeam tickles someone's nose,
While flip-flops dance on sea,
Each wave a chuckle rolling past,
In joyful jubilee.

The sun makes fun of all the hats,
That tourists wear so tall,
As boisterous waves play tag around,
And seagulls start to call.

Palm trees sway with laughter sweet,
In their tropical ballet,
While surfboards glide on comic tales,
Painting smiles in bright array.

With every splash and giddy wave,
Summer's hugs are bold,
In echoes of an embrace,
Where stories of joy are told.

The Kaleidoscope of a Tropical Evening

The colors swirl in laughter bright,
As night begins to hum,
A parrot cracks some silly jokes,
While palm trees sway and strum.

A ukulele joins the fun,
With plucky notes that tease,
The fireflies around play peek-a-boo,
Dancing in the breeze.

Laughter spills like coconut milk,
In shades of pink and gold,
As night wraps up the island sky,
With stories to be told.

The kaleidoscope of joy unfolds,
In laughter's warm embrace,
For every evening's dance and song,
Is wrapped in a playful trace.

The Sweet Song of Gentle Gales

Whispers play among the palms,
Coconuts fall with hilarious calms.
Seagulls squawk, a comic tune,
As sunburnt tourists chase their loons.

Flip-flops flop like fish out of sea,
While locals laugh at the clumsy spree.
Kites spin high, caught in a dance,
Who said their elegance lost all chance?

Umbrellas flip in the salty air,
As laughter goes soaring everywhere.
Sandy dogs prance, tails in a whirl,
It's a comedic chaos, watch it unfurl.

In the shadows of swaying trees,
Napping crabs dream beside the breeze.
Punters giggle, the view is grand,
What a funny way, to enjoy the sand!

Petals in the Coastal Mist

Petals tumble from the trees,
Caught in laughter with the breeze.
Tropical drinks spill on the floor,
As kids giggle, shout for more.

Shells start dancing on the shore,
As seagulls argue, who wants more?
Sandcastles crumble with a sigh,
Who said they'd last? They just fly by!

Fish on hooks are making a fuss,
"Why are we bait?" they grumble and cuss.
Lines tangled up like a yarn ball tease,
While fishermen chuckle, "We'll do as we please!"

So we toast with soda and cheer,
To silly moments we hold dear.
In the mist, where petals twirl,
Life's a slapstick, dizzying whirl!

Lullabies from the Edge of Paradise

Palm trees sway in a sleepy hum,
Laughter echoes, here we come!
Luau dancers trip on their feet,
A funny shuffle, can't be beat!

Tiki torches flicker with grace,
As pineapple hats bound to embrace.
A toucan drops its fruity treat,
While children giggle, "Hey, that's neat!"

Moonlit waves play hide and seek,
A crab wears shades, looking chic.
We sing along to the waves' soft lilt,
Making jokes as giggles build.

In this paradise, a nightly spell,
Comedic tales we love to tell.
With sleepy smiles as tactics wise,
Belly laughs under starry skies!

Sandcastles and Whirling Vows

Sandcastles rise with grandeur so bright,
But watch out! They burst with delight!
Kids build towers, then step back,
Water comes rushing, oh what a crack!

Seashells echo their giggling chat,
As a crab dons a tiny hat.
Weddings near the shoreline proceed,
As hiccuping bouquets don't quite succeed!

Waves crash in a joyful roar,
"Did someone order a bit more?"
Seaweed wigs make the sea life laugh,
While dolphins join in the silly staff.

With every tide, the sun will set,
But our goofy hearts won't forget.
In swirling vows, the laughter grows,
With sandcastles where love still flows!

Winds of Change in Coral Coves

A parrot squawks at the sun,
As flip-flops dance, just for fun.
Fishy tales on the shore,
Laughing waves beg for more.

Seagulls play tag in the sky,
While crabs scuttle, oh my!
The ocean winks at me now,
Who knew seaweed could take a bow?

The Wandering Heart of the Island

A coconut rolls, oh dear me,
Chasing palm trees like they're free.
Islanders chuckle and sigh,
As lizards leap, oh my, oh my!

The sun is clocked with a shell,
As turtles sing, what a swell!
Swaying hats in a flirtatious dance,
Island life's a merry chance.

A Serendipitous Windward Journey

Riding waves on a rubber raft,
A crab gives chase, he's quite daft!
Shells roll out like a curtain call,
Will someone catch them? Not at all!

In the shade of an old bamboo,
A rooster crows, just for you.
The waves and laughs then collide,
As the tide boasts its silly pride.

Canvas of Sky and Sea

Canvas colors swirling bright,
Fishing rods in silly sight.
Picnic ants tease the laid spread,
"Hey, where's the sandwich?" one said.

As kites soar on a merry run,
Children giggle, oh what fun!
The horizon smiles, could it be,
The sunset's snicker's for you and me?

Nature's Gentle Orchestra

A chicken plays the lute, oh what a sight,
While crickets dance, hopping left and right.
The cows wear shades, lounging by the stream,
While frogs in top hats croak a jazzy theme.

The flowers giggle, swaying in delight,
The sunflowers spin, oh what a flight!
A parrot cracks jokes, he's quite the star,
While ants take notes, dreaming of a car.

The clouds drift by, wearing silly grins,
Pigs on stilts perform, it's where the fun begins.
The ducks waddle on, their feathers in a twist,
Nature's laughter echoes, can't resist!

Under the canopy, the laughter shines,
Where every critter knows the best punchlines.
So join the fun, jolly and spry,
In this vivid world, our spirits fly.

The Whispering Leaves of Eden

The leaves hold secrets, whispering jokes,
As squirrels in hats make fun of the folks.
An owl cracks wise, perched high in a tree,
While mice in tuxedos sip tea with glee.

The flowers gossip, their petals all aglow,
As beetles tell tales of a wild dance show.
The sun winks down, a cheeky little chap,
As turtles in slippers take a brief nap.

The shadows stretch long, playing hide-and-seek,
While rabbits swap puns with a giggling squeak.
And oh, the wind joins in with a chuckle,
Tickling the grasses for a little shuffle.

In Eden's embrace, every chuckle rings,
Life's silly moments are simple things.
Join the sweet ruckus, dance to the tune,
In this land of laughter, we'll sing to the moon.

Sunlit Paths of Wind

The sun leads the way, with silly old rays,
Tickling the pathways in golden displays.
While shadows skip gladly, they dance on the ground,
And smiles grow wide with each tickle around.

The sand giggles softly, so warm and so bright,
While beach balls bounce by, oh what a sight!
Seagulls are swooping, stealing a fry,
As children all laugh and let out a cry.

The palm trees sway, with hats made of leaves,
Like joyful old grandpas, just pulling your sleeves.
Time rolls along like the waves on the shore,
Each moment filled with laughter, who could ask for more?

As day turns to dusk, the fun never wanes,
With stories of fish on the back of the trains.
So come take a stroll, the path's full of cheer,
With laughter and joy for everyone here.

Hush of the Tropic Night

The moon plays peek-a-boo, hiding behind,
While fireflies giggle, all links intertwined.
A lizard in pajamas struts on the wall,
As crickets compose a symphony for all.

The coconut whispers secrets of the day,
While gentle waves tease the night into play.
The stars twinkle brightly, they flash a good joke,
As owls hoot softly, a wise little poke.

The night air is filled with a playful charm,
As geckos will charm you with their sweet alarm.
The silvery laughter wraps snug and tight,
In this hush of the night, oh what a delight!

So dance with the shadows beneath the trees,
And join in the fun, let's all feel the breeze.
With night's lighthearted spirit, we soar and glide,
In this world full of giggles, let laughter abide.

Murmurs of a Hidden Cove

In the cove where laughter sings,
Seagulls dance on silly wings,
Tides tickle sandy toes,
While each mischievous wave just goes.

A crab in pajamas sprints away,
Chasing a jellyfish in disarray,
With shells for hats and laughter loud,
The fish form a giggling crowd.

A clam tells tales with a wink,
While octopuses join in to think,
What's more absurd, the sea or sand?
In this hilarious, aquatic land.

With every splash, a joke is told,
Mermaids giggle, both coy and bold,
It's hard to be serious, you'd agree,
When you're at the cove, wild and free.

Embrace of the Isle's Emotions

On a shore where laughter grows,
A parrot cracks jokes with a nose,
That somehow looks like a spoon,
It shares punchlines 'neath the moon.

Waves roll in like a playful dog,
Chasing its tail, a dancing fog,
The sun tickles with rays so bright,
As the seaweed sways, oh what a sight!

Lovers plant kisses on the sand,
While crabs perform in a marching band,
The heart hums tunes of love and glee,
As the tides whisper secrets, can't you see?

An island's embrace, both silly and sweet,
With coconuts rolling on tiny feet,
In this garden of whimsy where joy reigns,
Even the tortoises joke about their gains.

Currents of Calm

The waves tiptoe as they arrive,
With ticklish splashes to keep us alive,
A floaty seaweed waves goodbye,
To clammy crabs that love to fly.

A floating log with a grin so wide,
Makes sea turtles dance with pride,
While fish do pirouettes and flips,
Chasing bubbles on feathery hips.

The sunlight draws a funny face,
In a jellyfish's graceful trace,
As laughter echoes with each gentle roll,
A comedy captured in nature's scroll.

From sunsets with giggles to dawns with cheer,
The island plays tricks, never fear,
For in this paradise of joy and balm,
Every moment is perfectly calm.

A Romantic Zephyr

A gentle whisper from the tide,
Calls out for lovers to confide,
As sandcastles lean to hear the tale,
Of a seagull flying without fail.

Cupid's arrow, a buoy that floats,
Drawing hearts on adventurous boats,
Where seaweed crowns the lovers so fair,
They dance with the wind, light as air.

Shells sing sweetly, a chorus divine,
With giggles and grins, the stars align,
While the sun dips low in a rosy delight,
The dance of the waves is a comical sight.

So they twirl and spin, lost in the charm,
Of salty love with a hint of balm,
For every snicker and playful tease,
Makes the heart swell like the gentle breeze.

The Whispering Path of Clouds

Fluffy sheep roam the bright blue sky,
Fashioned by dreams and the winds that sigh.
One drifts low, snagging a coconut tree,
With its fluffy tail, it giggles with glee.

Up above, a parrot gives a loud squawk,
While the sun plays tag with the sneaky clock.
The clouds wear hats as they gather to chat,
Swapping tales of where the raindrops sat.

A rainbow slips on, much to clouds' surprise,
Declaring, 'I'm the star of the painted skies!'
But lightning's mood swings make everyone yelp,
As thunder proclaims, 'We've got storms to kelp!'

So on they frolic, with a wink and a twist,
Finding fun in each swirl, they cannot resist.
Life's a merry dance when the weather is fair,
On this path of whispers, we float on a prayer.

Shores Adrift in Time's Touch

The beach toys gossip, washed up on the sand,
Claiming to be the best in all of the land.
A bucket shouts, 'I'm the ultimate king!'
While a shovel laughs, 'Nope, I'm the bling!'

Seagulls debate on the freshest of fries,
As a crab scuttles, sneaking curious spies.
Shells giggle softly, crafting love letters,
While a sly fish sneaks in, catching the setters.

The tide bounces back with a playful slap,
As flippers and whirls swirl in a clap.
The sun gets jealous, losing best tan,
To the squawking raccoon with a beachy plan.

They dance with the waves, and the foam dives low,
Creating a giggle, while the seaweed grows.
A day filled with laughter, under the sky's watch,
At shores adrift in the tide's merry swatch.

Threads of Gold in the Ocean's Tapestry

Goldfish wear crowns, strutting in the sea,
Flashing their teeth, feeling wild and free.
The kelp sways gently, swishing to the beat,
As the starfish revels in each sandy retreat.

Seashells whisper secrets of old pirate dreams,
Playing hide and seek under sunlit beams.
An octopus teaches some wild dance moves,
While the clownfish laughs, making funny grooves.

A shipwrecked anchor busts out its flair,
Telling tall tales to the curious air.
With tales of treasures and battles galore,
In this tapestry, legends wash ashore.

So swim with a laugh, let giggles unfold,
As threads of the ocean weave stories of gold.
From bubbles to splashes, the fun's always here,
In the aquatic realm, we dance without fear.

Mists of Memories at Dusk

When the sun dips low, the shadows prance,
The trees join in a whimsical dance.
A rabbit in glasses checks time with a clock,
While frogs in tuxedos croak 'What a shock!'

The fog rolls in with a fuzzy embrace,
Hiding shy crabs that scuttle in place.
A squirrel spins tales of acorns galore,
As otters crowd 'round, craving humor and more.

Cuddly critters play tricks on the moon,
Whispering jokes, giggling out of tune.
The stars look down, twinkling with glee,
At the merry night scene, chaos set free.

So welcome the dusk, with memories bright,
Where laughter and silliness fuddle the night.
With joy in our hearts, we remember to play,
For the mists of today are tomorrow's ballet.

Secrets Carried by the Sea

The fish whispered tales, oh so sly,
Of sunken treasures that make sailors cry.
Seagulls gossip, they dive and squawk,
While crabs hold parties, they dance on the dock.

Shells keep secrets, nestled in sand,
Conch shells giggle at things they've planned.
The waves chuckle loud, as they tickle the shore,
Playing hide and seek, we all want more!

Dance of the Salty Air

Windy narwhals are twirling about,
With dolphin partners who leap and shout.
Even the sun has a twinkling grin,
Bouncing to rhythms the ocean spins.

Kites fly up, catching the breeze,
While chubby crabs do the funniest tease.
Ocean spray giggles, splashing the crew,
In a whimsical waltz, it's a watery zoo!

Harmony with Nature's Breath

Palm fronds sway like they're brushing their hair,
While turtles join in with their slow, funny flair.
The sun plays peek-a-boo with the clouds above,
And the waves clap hands as if in love.

Pelicans dance with their big beaks in sync,
Painting the sky, oh what do you think?
Nature's a joker, it plays with delight,
In the party of life, it shines so bright!

Swaying Palms and Serene Skies

Coconuts whisper their fondest dreams,
While the breeze makes ruckus with giggling streams.
Palm trees lean close, sharing their tales,
Of sun-soaked adventures and wind-filled gales.

Butterflies flutter, wearing their best,
Playing tag with the bees, a fun little quest.
Under the sun, life's a playful ride,
With nature laughing, let's sway with pride!

Mosaic of the Island's Heart

On the shore, the seagulls squawk,
Dancing like they're on a clock.
A crab in a top hat struts around,
Thinking he's the king, so proud.

Shells are winking in the sun,
'Hey there, tourists, come have fun!'
With cada cactus gossiping cheer,
They spill the tea, loud enough to hear.

Sandy toes and flip-flop claps,
While jellyfish plan ocean maps.
The sun's a jester, bright and bold,
Telling tales that never get old.

A coconut tumbles with a laugh,
Rolling on its merry path.
Here, the island's heart swells with glee,
In a mosaic of quirks, wild and free.

The Tale of Windswept Shores

Oh, the winds that twist and twirl,
Making hats fly off in a whirl!
The locals laugh as the kite takes flight,
Bobbing like a clumsy dinosaur's fright.

Margaritas spill with a splash,
As umbrellas flip in a dash.
'Catch me if you can!' they tease,
As the ocean giggles with a breeze.

Fish on bikes zoom past the sand,
A strange parade by the water's strand.
The sun can't help but wink and play,
Joining the fun in this silly fray.

In the tale of shores so bright,
Laughter echoes into the night.
With each jest and jokey cheer,
Life is a party, come grab a beer!

Whispers of the Coastal Wind

The whispers weave through palm tree leaves,
Chattering secrets and funny thieves.
A clam with glasses reads the tide,
Crafting jokes that cannot hide.

Octopuses juggle with a flair,
As fish play cards without a care.
'High tide, low tide, it's all the same,'
Said the crab, puffing up with fame.

Flip-flops printed with silly rhyme,
Declare it's party time, no crime!
The breeze then twirls like a capering ghost,
Tickling quaint islands, laughing the most.

Among the whispers of salty air,
Every cheeky tale, we gladly share.
In this coastal land of shades and spins,
Life is a joke; let the laughter begin!

Starlit Shores and Gentle Currents

At starlit shores where laughter glows,
The moon wears shades, and the ocean knows.
Starfish dancing to a beachy beat,
With conch shells clapping in joyful heat.

The gentle current winks from afar,
Sneaking up to tickle your car!
While jellyfish sport their glowing dress,
Playing hide and seek, oh what a mess!

Sandcastles rise like wobbly dreams,
While crabs contend for summer teams.
Beach balls fly with a loud 'Whee!'
The night air ripples with glee in spree.

With every wave that crashes ashore,
There's a giggle hidden down to the core.
Starlit shores, what a whimsical blast,
With gentle currents that never seem to last.

The Melody of Floating Dreams

A coconut danced with a silly grin,
Waves giggled softly, chuckling within.
Palm trees swayed in a ballet of cheer,
As flip-flops soared through the atmosphere.

Seagulls in shades, taking selfies on cliffs,
While crabs play tag, making wild, funny shifts.
Sun hats flipped off in a playful fight,
As laughter rang out beneath the bright light.

A sunburned tourist, looking quite bold,
Decides to make sand angels, all covered in gold.
The beach ball bounces, a mischievous sprite,
Sending beach goers into a hilarious flight.

At night, the fireflies joined a funky parade,
Illuminate the dance floor, all glitter and shade.
The waves join the chorus with a wet slap,
While everyone giggles at the silly mishap.

Secrets of Seashells and Soft Winds

Seashells whisper secrets in a curious tone,
Of pirates and treasures, and laughter they've sown.
A starfish is plotting to host a grand ball,
With jellyfish floaters, oh, they'll have a ball!

Turtles in bowties, waltzing with grace,
While clams share the gossip of this silly place.
The ocean hums tunes of ticklish delight,
As the tide plays tricks on the moon's silver light.

A sea cucumber jokes, "I'm the fanciest dish!"
While crabs roll their eyes at this mismatched swish.
The sand tickles toes as the seashells all giggle,
While dolphins pop up, making everyone wiggle.

Manta rays dance, in their stylish fine gear,
Belly laughing softly just to spread that good cheer.
With every soft wave that tickles the shore,
Seashells keep chuckling and always want more.

Embracing the Essence of Paradise

In the heart of bliss where the sun takes a dip,
A pineapple winks from its tropical trip.
With each splash of color, the laughter erupts,
As sunscreened humans attempt the best jumps.

A hammock sways gently, holding two cakes,
While toddlers concoct enormous sand lakes.
Each wave carries joy on its foamy curls,
And all the seagulls sport colorful pearls.

An octopus chef flipping burgers in haste,
While flamingos prance with a fashionable taste.
Oh, laughter erupts like the waves that do crash,
As sunburns and giggles create quite the splash.

Beach balls are flying, like wild little birds,
Two kids play dodgeball, with laughter, not words.
In this quirky haven of spirits so free,
Paradise chuckles—won't you join the spree?

A Serenade of Island Dreams

The ukulele strums as the palms sway and sway,
Monkeys swing by, what a curious display!
A flamingo dances with a hat far too big,
While the tide tickles toes, hiding shells in a jig.

Toast to the coconuts, cheers! They reply,
With roasted beach laughter soaring up high.
A conch shell recites the best dad jokes around,
As waves leap with glee, joyfully unbound.

The sunset is blushing, giving high fives,
While crabs in tuxedos show off their wise lives.
"Let's dance on the shore!" hollers a merry fish,
With dreams made of jelly, they swish and they swish.

So grab your sandals, let's hop down the sand,
Join this wild serenade, it's perfectly grand!
With whimsy and wonder, let's raise a toast loud,
For moments of laughter, let's all be proud!

Memories Carried on the Wind

A sandwich flew past my nose,
With mayo that slathered my toes.
The seagulls squawked in delight,
Catching crumbs in a playful flight.

Laughter danced on the ocean's face,
As I ran in a wild, mad race.
A lifeguard's hat took to the sky,
Leaving me with a puzzled sigh.

Shells giggled softly on the sand,
Whispers of stories, oh so grand.
Each wave a jest, a tiny prank,
That left me grinning, by the bank.

The sun winked down with a cheeky ray,
It was a perfect, silly day.
With memories wrapped in seaweed's twist,
I'd laugh again, oh how I missed!

The Island's Silent Song

The palm trees swayed with a grin,
In the breeze where the mischief begins.
Coconuts dropped with a thud,
Creating a symphony of fun and mud.

A crab in a tuxedo dashed by,
With a swagger and a wild, bold cry.
He twirled in the sand, oh what a sight,
The island danced under moonlight.

Turtles played peekaboo with the tide,
Waves chuckled, in a playful ride.
Each ripple a hint of a joke untold,
The ocean's secrets were pure gold.

Seagulls juggled shells like clowns,
Their antics brought giggles from towns.
In this harmony of stone and sea,
The island's laughter was wild and free.

Shadows Under the Canopy

In the shade, where laughter hides,
The mischief of monkeys abides.
They swing and they chatter, in playful cheer,
Turning simple strolls into a comic seer.

A squirrel wore sunglasses like a star,
Thinking 'I'm the coolest by far!'
But tripped on a vine, in a silly flop,
Sending acorns flying, a giggling crop.

Under the leaves, light plays on the ground,
With shadows that dance, round and round.
Each step a chuckle, a twist and a turn,
In this jungle of joy, there's much to learn.

The breeze carries tales of vine and root,
Of quirky creatures that share their loot.
Every sound, a narrative we keep,
In this canopy of laughter, so deep.

Patterns of Light and Air

Sunbeams scattered, a playful game,
Creating patterns, never the same.
A kite went soaring with a cheeky flip,
   Its tail a trail in a hacky trip.

Fish splashed and chuckled at passerby,
With each tiny splash, they'd wink and fly.
While flip-flops danced, lost on the way,
   A lost little shoe began to sway.

Colors bright in the azure scene,
With laughter embroidered in shades of green.
Tropical breezes, a ticklish tease,
Carried whispers of silly degrees.

With faces aglow in the golden light,
We laughed until stars took their flight.
For every moment, a quirky delight,
In patterns of joy, we felt so right.

Conversations with the Horizon

I asked the sun, 'How's your day?'
It chuckled loud, then faded away.
The clouds joined in with their fluffy glee,
Said, 'We've got places to float and see.'

The waves chimed in, a splashing jest,
'Guess we're the ones who do it best!'
A gull squawked loud, 'Don't forget me!'
Then, swooped down low, so fancy and free!

The palm trees swayed, gossiping fast,
'Who's the bold one that's filled with sass?'
Each gust of wind carried their tales,
Of crabs in suits, and fish in pails.

As twilight fell with a twinkling grin,
The horizon winked, ready to spin.
In laughter, we found where spirits align,
Conversations merged, oh, how divine!

The Wind's Intimate Secrets

The wind whispering, secrets untold,
Of coconut dreams and sandcastles bold.
It teased the palm leaves with silly gags,
Got tangled in laughter, while playing like rags.

'The ocean's a joker,' it giggled with glee,
'He tickles the shore, can't you see?'
A clam once claimed, 'I'm the king of this land!'
While a starfish pirouetted on fine golden sand.

Jellyfish floated with a graceful cheer,
Who knew being soggy could spread such good cheer?
The wind, like a prankster, darted around,
Turning stiff moments to giggly sound.

With whispers and laughs, it sped through the pines,
Leaving behind maps of invisible lines.
A secret revealed, in a chuckle it weaves,
The island's alive with all of its leaves!

Kaleidoscope of Sky and Ocean

The sky painted hues like a wild kids' game,
Splashing colors on water, never the same.
A fish winked, 'Look at my new shiny scales!'
As seagulls debated their grand lunchtime tales.

'What's for dinner?' the pelican teased,
'Zero-calorie sandwiches, if you're pleased!'
The ocean just giggled, imitating glee,
With wave after wave in a rhythmic spree.

Sunset arrived with a sly little grin,
Mirroring mischief, to tease out the win.
The clouds danced around, in whimsical flight,
Like cotton candy spun under the twilight.

The stars blinked awake, ready for fun,
Outshining the moon, like it's just begun.
In this view of wonder, with laughter we plummet,
An island of giggles, how lucky we summon!

Driftwood Dreams and Twilight Whispers

On driftwood dreams, we build our castles,
With twigs as towers and shells as vassals.
The tide rolled in, with a playful nudge,
While we called it fancy, the wave gave a grudge.

Crabs held court, in a shell-held throne,
Debating if beach naps should overblown.
From laughter and grumbles, the seagulls chimed,
A serenade of silliness, perfectly timed.

Twilight whispered, 'Let's soften this light!'
As shadows grew longer, in the softening night.
Fish were playing hide-and-seek in the dark,
While we built stories, igniting a spark.

How silly it seems, this life far from haste,
With grins that catch time, in delicate taste.
Driftwood dreams wrapping us in soft embrace,
Twilight giggles ushering us into space!

Echoes of Laughter on Calm Waters

The seagulls squawk, a comic tune,
While crab and clam share words by noon.
A fish with a hat swims right on by,
And dolphins giggle in the sky.

The waves wear smiles, a playful dance,
As children splash in a summer trance.
Sunbathers chuckle with ice cream cones,
While seaweed tickles jellyfish bones.

Just past the pier, a dog does a leap,
Chasing shells that won't let him creep.
Laughter echoes, carrying far,
As flip-flops fly beneath the bar.

The tide rolls in with a wobbly grin,
Bringing in tales where chuckles begin.
Here fun is found, and joy's at play,
On shores where silliness paves the way.

The Artistry of Driftwood and Waves

A stick came floating, dressed in grime,
A masterpiece, lost to time.
He poses grand, like ancient art,
While the shore giggles, playing its part.

The old flip-flop tells wild tales,
Of beach volleyball and epic fails.
The tide agrees with a rollicking cheer,
As sandcastles quake—oh dear, oh dear!

Barnacles sit with their polished hats,
Swapping stories with strolling cats.
The shells roll by, each wanting fame,
In this sea sitcom, oh what a game!

As daylight fades, the stars appear,
Each one a wink, a snicker, a cheer.
The night plays tricks with shadows low,
A comedy show put on by the flow.

Flourishes of Nature's Caress

Waves toss seaweed like confetti bright,
As crabs compete in a chuckle fight.
Sand doves prance, fluffing their tails,
While one silly gull slips on snails.

The palm trees sway, a dance so grand,
Telling stories of a soft, sweet land.
Coconuts chuckle, they take a fall,
As laughter lingers, echoing all.

Fish flash smiles beneath the tide,
While laughing clams try to hide.
Bubbles float, each a giggling gem,
A secret world where whimsy stems.

Each nook and cranny holds a jest,
Where nature blooms in its playful quest.
Oh, what a joy to live and play,
With the ocean's touch guiding the way!

Kisses of the Ocean's Breath

The tide whispers jokes to the sandy shore,
As splashy surprises begin to soar.
Starfish dance on a soap bubble boat,
While green sea turtles giggle and float.

Flip-flops squeak like ducks in a line,
Trying to step in perfect time.
With each wave's swell, a playful shout,
As laughter lingers, casting doubt.

The fish wear bow ties for a fancy show,
While jellyfish waltz with an elegant flow.
Barnacle buddies share cheesy grins,
Capturing memories where laughter begins.

The night brings out winks from stars on high,
Sharing secrets, oh my, oh my!
With each little crackle and whispering wave,
Joy flows freely, all hearts it'll save.

Echoes of the Ocean's Lullaby

Waves giggle as they kiss the shore,
Seagulls squawk, demanding more.
Crabs dance sideways, wearing a beat,
While sandcastles shuffle their tiny feet.

The sun's a jester, paintbrush in hand,
Tickling the sky, a colorful land.
Flip-flops flapping, a toe-tapping sound,
Even the seaweed sways all around.

Shells whisper secrets of underwater dreams,
Turtles play poker, or so it seems.
A jellyfish giggles, floating away,
As children laugh, soaking up the play.

Under the sun, time's laughter rings clear,
Island antics bring joy, never a fear.
The ocean's a stage, it keeps the score,
As we lose track, never wanted more.

Secrets of a Sunlit Serenity

Sunbeams dance like they've lost their mind,
Tickling the palm trees, they unwind.
Sandy toes wriggle, living the dream,
While coconuts plot a ridiculous scheme.

A parrot squawks jokes from high in the sky,
Whispering tales that make dolphins cry.
Tanning turtles share sunbathing tips,
As the sand squirts laughter from tiny slips.

Laughter erupts from a beach ball's bounce,
While flip-flops flounder, you can hear them clounce.
The sun's bright grin, shines wide and free,
A clownish crag in this comic spree.

In this land where giggles never cease,
Even the sea seems to smile with ease.
Nature's humor's a playful affair,
Each golden moment traps joy in the air.

The Driftwood's Tale

Once a mighty tree, now a beach's delight,
Driftwood tells stories beneath the moonlight.
He chuckles at gulls, claiming the spotlight,
And heckles the waves jousting left and right.

With a twist and a turn, he tries hard to dance,
But his roots are long gone, he's lost in the trance.
Sunburnt and happy, he plays every part,
As beachgoers bring him their best joke chart.

Every grain of sand shares a giggling tale,
Of pirates and mermaids that set out to sail.
His wooden grains hold laughter and glee,
In this comedy of nature, wacky and free.

So when you walk by, toss a wink his way,
Join in the fun; he'll brighten your day.
This driftwood is wise, with a grin so wide,
A jester of the shore, where joy can't hide.

Twilight Touch on the Water's Edge

As twilight drops its curtain, fireflies ignite,
Splashing stars on the canvas, oh what a sight!
The water chuckles, tickled by the light,
While gnarled old mangroves dance just right.

Bats flit about in a comical chase,
While frogs in tuxedos croak with grace.
The wind's a prankster, teasing the reeds,
Making even the shyest of shells take leads.

A crab with a hat sets out for a stroll,
He tips his way past the skipping shoal.
With laughter echoing off the rocks so near,
Every splash tells a joke for the ear.

As the evening glimmers in playful delight,
Nature hums softly, all wrongs made right.
In this whimsical world where humor prevails,
The twilight winks, spinning delightful tales.

The Quiet Caress of Dusk

As sun dips low, the seagulls squawk,
Shells roll in like a bad knock-knock.
The waves tickle toes, but watch your drink,
Seaweed wigs might just make you blink.

A crab plays tag, with a curious look,
Swags its claws like it's in a book.
The sand slips through with each silly laugh,
Imagine creatures plotting a photograph.

Palm trees sway, looking for a snack,
Mangoes tumble — it's a crazy hack.
All while the moon grins down its prize,
Tiny fish zoom, and they all rise.

So as dusk falls in this wild charade,
I give a toast to the fun parade!
May laughs ripple like the playful sea,
As we dance with joy, so wild and free.

Feathered Thoughts on the Horizon

Parrots wear hats, quite the display,
Screeching secrets in a feathery way.
A pelican drops its lunch with a splash,
Crustacean critters just run and dash.

Kites soar high, while kids run about,
Chasing after dreams — without a doubt!
The ocean giggles, with each little splash,
Sending giggles upwards in a joyful crash.

Each day's a circus of winged delight,
With toucans who dance and giggle at night.
Waves clap their hands, while gulls take a bow,
As if they're saying, "Look at us now!"

So let's not forget in all of this fun,
Those feathered thoughts that fly just like the sun.
With laughter unending, we'll share what we find,
In the dance of the sea, we leave cares behind.

Tides of Tranquility

The tide rolls in with a cheeky grin,
Playing tag with toes — oh, where to begin?
Each wave whispers jokes in soft sand-end,
Even the starfish seem to pretend.

Sun hats flip in the wind's playful tease,
As kids build castles, wobbly like cheese.
Even the flip-flops start to conspire,
Jumping waves with a splashy desire!

Sandy snacks get shared with a cheer,
But watch those gulls — they're crafty, my dear!
With each crunch-crunch, laughter rebounds,
As the ocean keeps track of our goofy sounds.

So here's a toast to the tides that play,
To the smiles that last, come what may.
May our hearts be light, like a leaf in the sea,
As we dance with each wave, as wild as can be!

Moonglow on Tropical Dreams

The moon pops up like a cheeky chap,
Casting shadows on a sunken map.
Crickets start singing their late-night song,
While mischief dances, all night long.

Coconuts grin from their leafy perch,
Imitating folks who attend the search.
The night is alive with laughter and cheer,
As critters plan parties, far and near.

Glowworms light paths, guiding our way,
With tippy-toe secrets they softly sway.
The ocean hums tunes of frolic and fun,
Under the gaze of a mischievous sun.

So here's to the dreams on a tropical night,
Where laughter of creatures feels just right.
With each wave a giggle and each breeze a beam,
Let's dance like the stars in this whimsical dream.

A Symphony of Seaglass Whispers

In a world of seaglass dreams,
The funny fish just swim in teams.
They wear old hats, they laugh and sing,
While crabs do the cha-cha, it's quite a thing.

The clams are plotting with the waves,
Creating jigs and silly graves.
With every splash, a giggle floats,
As seagulls dance in bright pink coats.

At sunset's brush, they faintly sway,
A merry band in a salty bay.
With each soft wave, a chuckle shared,
As seashells whisper secrets bared.

So come along the shore with me,
And watch the shenanigans, oh so free!
In this glassy world, we'll lose all care,
For laughter's magic fills the air.

The Soft Kiss of Saltwater

When salty kisses greet my feet,
I giggle as the waves retreat.
The starfish wink, the sand crabs race,
In this comical, sunny place.

A jellyfish jigs, a crab does prance,
Who knew this sea could do the dance?
While clumsy dolphins flip and flop,
Splashing all the folks, oh what a drop!

Seashells gossip as they spin,
While seaweed wraps around a fin.
I swear, the octopus is sly,
With eight arms waving, oh my, oh my!

So come and dip your toes in fun,
Where pranks are played and laughter spun.
With each soft splash, a grin appears,
As salty kisses dry our fears.

Island Melodies on the Wind

The wind hums tunes of joy and glee,
As palm trees sway with playful glee.
The parrots squawk, a chatty lot,
While monkeys tease and share their pot.

A ukulele strums a silly beat,
While turtles groove with polka feet.
With every note, a chuckle flies,
As dolphins tease the passing skies.

Waves clap along, a rhythm divine,
As laughter sparkles like good wine.
From fishy jokes to birdy cheer,
The island sings, come lend an ear!

So join the dance, don't be shy,
Come sway with me beneath the sky.
With melodies that swirl and spin,
Our merry hearts shall surely win!

Shadows Beneath the Coconut Trees

Underneath the coconut shade,
The shadows dance, a grand parade.
Bumbling goats trip on their hooves,
While giggling kids make silly moves.

A crab in a hat, so full of sass,
Winks at a dog who's got the class.
As coconuts drop with thudding sound,
The audience laughs from all around.

In this theatre of nature's play,
Where lizards bask and frolic away.
With every rustle, a joke is spun,
As warm sunlight shimmers, oh what fun!

So sit awhile, let laughter swell,
With shadows and smiles, all is well.
Beneath these trees, life's a breeze,
Let's savor the joy, as we please.

Windswept Memories

On a gnarled tree, a parrot sat,
With a strong opinion on this and that.
He squawked and flapped, mistook my hat,
As I chased him round, now how 'bout that!

The sand flew high, twirling in delight,
As I stumbled and tumbled, not quite upright.
A crab danced near with a sideways glance,
I swear he chuckled at my mischance!

A turtle swam by wearing my shirt,
He paused for a laugh, left me in the dirt.
With every gust, my plans went awry,
Who knew wind could be such a sly guy?

I gather my things, just a trifle askew,
With sand in my shoes and seaweed too.
Now that's how I'll remember this day,
Laughter and chaos, what more can I say?

Gentle Touch of Nature's Hand

The palm trees danced like they owned the place,
I tried to join in, but lost all grace.
A sneaky gust swept my sandwich away,
Leaving only crumbs for the gulls at play.

The sun wore shades like a star at a show,
While flip-flops flopped with a zany flow.
I joked with a seagull, he cawed back right,
As my sunglasses took off, oh, what a sight!

A hammock swung loose in a wild, wild way,
I tried for a nap, but the wind had its say.
With a whoosh and a swish, I fell to the ground,
Nature's touch knows how to fool around!

I chuckle with joy, as I dust off my rear,
The island's got quirks that just bring cheer.
With every gust, I find a new friend,
In nature's hand, the fun never ends!

The Harmony of Resounding Waves

Waves rolled in with a giggle and splash,
I leapt to escape, but my foot made a crash.
Fish leapt out, like they were on cue,
"Hey buddy, save some fun for us too!"

A beach ball soared like a kite in the air,
It bounced off my head, oh, what a flare!
The ocean's chorus, a hilarity jam,
With each little wave, they all went wham!

I danced with the tide, a true merman's dance,
But the ripples and frolics had me in a trance.
The sea laughed along, with a wink and a cheer,
"Stay close, dear friend, we're in for a year!"

So here by the shore, let the laughter persist,
With waves as my band, I can't resist.
For in every splash, there's a joke to be found,
In the harmony of waves, joy knows no bound!

Embracing the Ocean's Embrace

The ocean's arms wrapped around my feet,
Tickling my toes, a ticklish treat!
With a snicker the tide pulled back in a rush,
I yelped in surprise, "Oh, you cheeky hush!"

A starfish drifted like a friendly guide,
Showing off moves to the crabs that abride.
I tried to join in with a jig of my own,
But ended up tangled, oh, how I'd groan!

Seagulls squawked jokes as they flew overhead,
"Why did the clam flip? It was in a bed!"
With laughter and laughter, the kelp swung along,
While I danced the worm to their silly song.

As the sun set low, I felt quite at home,
With waves and wide smiles, I'd never more roam.
In the ocean's embrace, I found my free place,
Where fun has no limits and joy sets the pace!

Whispers of the Coastal Wind

Seagulls squawking, quite the show,
They steal my fries, oh no, oh no!
The sand is hot, I jump around,
In flip-flops, I trip—oh, where's the ground?

A crab in my bucket, what's he doing here?
He's got a plan, I start to fear.
He dances a jig, pinches my toe,
In my beach chair, I'm laughing low.

Flip-flops flying, it's all a chase,
Chasing laughter in this sunny place.
My hat takes off, it's gone with the gust,
Like my dignity, in the sand it's thrust!

Drinks in hand, we toast with glee,
Cheers to the sun and the salty spree.
With each gust, we're light and free,
Just don't ask me where my phone could be!

Dance of the Ocean's Breath

The waves are laughing, a silly sound,
Tickling toes as I flop around.
A jellyfish floats, quite out of place,
It waves hello—ah, what a face!

My snorkel's leaking, that's a thrill,
As I splash about like a fishy quill.
Mermaids giggle, they're in a swim,
With seaweed hair, oh, it's quite a whim!

We build a castle, it's fit for kings,
With moats of water and jellyfish rings.
But here comes the tide, the sea's a tease,
Our fortress crumbles with watery ease!

Ice cream drips from my sandy hand,
A seagull's eyeing it, oh isn't he grand?
With laughter echoing through the night,
I wipe my face, oh what a sight!

Secrets Carried by Salted Air

Tales of pirates and sunken gold,
Whispered secrets, legends bold.
A dog steals my sandwich, oh what a thief,
While my friends howl in shared disbelief!

My sunscreen's gone, it's quite the crime,
I'm all red now, but a monster of lime.
My hat's a sail, oh look at it go,
Blown by the wind—what a circus show!

Beach volleyball? I'm in the game!
But every serve causes utter shame.
Smacking the sand more than the ball,
Yet still, we're laughing, we've got a ball!

As the sun dips low, we gather round,
Sharing stories, with laughter abound.
With hearts like kites in the salty air,
I toss my worries, for joy, we share!

The Gentle Caress of Dusk

As the sun sets, the sky's a splash,
Pink and orange in colorful clash.
A fish jumped high, landed on me,
Now I smell like seafood, oh joy, oh glee!

Bonfire crackles, we roast some s'mores,
But watch out for sparks—who opens the doors?
The smoke's a dancer, swirling with flair,
While marshmallows burn, we laugh and stare.

My friend's on a quest, for the perfect shell,
But slips on the sand, oh what the hell!
With giggles erupting, I can't catch my breath,
In the end, he finds one—quite a death!

As evening closes, we sing our song,
Voices echoing, all night long.
With goofy grins and hearts so true,
Here's to moments, just me and you!

www.ingramcontent.com/pod-product-compliance
Lightning Source LLC
Chambersburg PA
CBHW072222070526
44585CB00015B/1450

Moonlit Secrets of the Sandy Cove

The moon played tag with the sandy shore,
Crabs did the cha-cha, oh what a score!
Fish wore sunglasses, think they're so cool,
While turtles debate 'What's the best pool?'

Stars twinkled brightly, a cosmic ballet,
Seagulls complained, 'What a weird cabaret!'
A beach ball soared to the rhythm of fun,
While jellyfish grinned, 'We're still number one!'

Reflections in Azure Waters

In waters so blue, a fish took a dive,
Swimming in circles, said, 'I'm alive!'
Pelicans laughed, with beaks open wide,
While starfish conspired to cause a tide.

The sun winks down, giving all a grin,
As shrimp practice dance moves, none look like him.
The seaweed hums tunes, a watery song,
While otters roll over, just playing along!

The Dance of the Salted Air

Waves wiggled in rhythm, the shore shook with glee,
As seagulls strummed tunes on a salty spree.
Sandcastles giggled with sand-sculpted glee,
While crabs wore top hats, 'Tis a grand jubilee!

The air was a dancehall of fragrant delight,
With beach balls a-bouncin', what a funny sight!
A concert of laughter, with each ocean roar,
As dolphins played kazoo from a coral shore!

Secrets Guarded by Ancient Rocks

Old rocks told stories of pirates and gold,
But they chuckled and said, 'We're better off cold!'
Eels in tuxedos planned a grand soiree,
While clams whispered secrets, all night and day.

Octopus showed off with his stylish flair,
While a crab clapped hands, his dance was quite rare.
Echoes of laughter flew high in the air,
As the tide shared tales that none could compare!

Dreams among the Palms

In the shade of swaying trees,
The monkeys hide and tease their knees.
A crab on a mission, oh what a sight,
Wiggles sideways, trying with all its might.

The coconuts gossip up high and loud,
While birds practice singing to impress the crowd.
A lizard slips, takes a tumble, a funny fall,
Just another day with laughter for all.

Echoes of the Coral Reef

The fish have formed a conga line,
Dancing through bubbles, oh so divine.
A clam in the corner sings bold and strong,
With pearls for notes, it can't go wrong.

A turtle named Frank loves a bit of fun,
He tries to race, but he's slower than none.
The octopus juggles, with style and grace,
In this underwater circus, who can keep pace?

A Dance of Moonlit Tides

The moon winks down on a shrimp in a suit,
Who dances alone, oh, what a hoot!
Stars twinkle in rhythm, a cosmic cheer,
While the waves clap along, what a sight here!

A glowing jelly slides by with a grin,
Belting out tunes, she wants to win.
The sand crabs clap, creating a beat,
As the night comes alive, oh, what a treat!

Beneath Celestial Canopies

The coconuts giggle when the wind starts to blow,
As if sharing secrets that only they know.
A parrot declares, with feathers so bright,
That he's the king of this silly night!

Meanwhile, a sandcastle looks tall and proud,
Until a wave crashes, drawing a crowd.
"Who built this thing?" the tiny crabs shout,
As they scurry away, filled with doubt!

Journeys in the Twilight Seas

On a boat made of cheese,
With a crew of dancing bees,
We sailed through jelly waves,
In search of pie-shaped caves.

The captain wore a hat,
Made of butter and a cat,
He claimed he knew the way,
To find the land of sway.

The fish all juggled cards,
While seagulls played guitars,
We laughed until we cried,
With our goofy nautical pride.

When the stars began to twirl,
And the waves began to whirl,
We anchored in a dream,
Where silly things could gleam.

The Language of the Salted Air

In a world where whispers play,
The wind told jokes all day,
Seashells giggled with delight,
Under the moon's silly light.

The sand said, "How do you do?"
As the waves wore socks of blue,
Crabs danced with a funny flair,
In the language of the air.

A parrot squawked with sass,
While we sipped from a glass,
Of lemonade that sparkled bright,
With a twist of giggles in the night.

Among the clouds so puffy, fun,
We laughed till we saw the sun,
As the tide tickled our toes,
In the breeze, the perfect prose.

Passionate Hues in the Evening Sky

As the sun said its goodbye,
The colors made us sigh,
With shades that winked and winked,
And painted clouds that blinked.

The pinks and purples danced,
While the blues hopped and pranced,
We wore hats made of rays,
And marveled at their plays.

A flamingo on a swing,
Sang songs of silly things,
With a ukulele bright,
They serenaded the night.

Under this laughter's hue,
The world felt fresh and new,
With giggles as our guide,
In the twilight, we would glide.

The Tangle of Roots and Stars

Roots of trees twisted tight,
Whispering secrets at night,
While the stars played hide-and-seek,
In a game that felt so cheek.

The moon wore a funny grin,
As the owls joined in the din,
They hooted jokes, oh what a sight,
In the tangled, starry light.

We climbed up the branches high,
And waved at clouds passing by,
With a squirrel juggling nuts,
And a raccoon in cute struts.

Amidst the roots and leaves,
Were laughter and silly thieves,
Stealing joy from night's embrace,
In this merry, magical place.

The Enchantment of Coral Gardens

In the depths where fish can laugh,
Coral castles have a giraffe.
Turtles dance with mighty grace,
While starfish play in a slow race.

Seashells gossip, tales unfold,
Bubbles burst with secrets bold.
Anemones throw a wild bash,
Where clowns swim in a quirky clash.

Treasure chests of pirate's dreams,
Filled with jelly and funny schemes.
Octopus serves drinks with flair,
As seahorses twirl without a care.

In this realm, all worries cease,
Where laughter floats, and joy's a feast.
Coral gardens, shine and sway,
The ocean's charm, in a playful display.

Underneath the Aurora of Waves

Jellyfish glow in rainbow hues,
Dancing like they've drunk the booze.
Crabs pinch with a comic twist,
While mermaids laugh, they can't resist.

Seaweed sways, much like a wig,
Fish in outfits do a jig.
Stars above and shells below,
Offer jokes that make us glow.

Surfers ride on bubbles bold,
In a world that's bright and gold.
Seals serenade with a croon,
As dolphins play beneath the moon.

Waves roll in with a cheerful clap,
Each splash tells a funny chap.
Underneath, a show of glee,
In waters deep, there's mystery.

The Colors of Dusk at Sea

As the sun dips down with glee,
The fish wave bye, "Come dance with me!"
Clouds wear pink, like cotton candy,
While a grouper's face looks quite dandy.

The horizon bursts in orange blaze,
With pirate ships that strut and gaze.
Seagulls squawk their funny song,
In every note, they can't go wrong.

Twilight brings a magic show,
Where polka-dots are all aglow.
A whale plays hide and seek with flair,
As shrimps line up, with jokes to share.

Undercover, the night begins,
With crabs telling notorious sins.
In the colors of dusk so neat,
The ocean giggles, oh so sweet.

Secrets Lurking Under the Surface

A clam hides secrets in its shell,
Whispers tales, it knows quite well.
Octopuses plot in clever schemes,
While seahorses giggle at their dreams.

Starfish swap stories, oh so sly,
While urchins pretend to be shy.
In coral nooks, the secrets keep,
As fish share jokes beneath the deep.

The current flows with a playful grin,
It teases crabs with a sly spin.
Eels play peek-a-boo with a twist,
In this dance of the ocean mist.

So listen close, for laughter's near,
In the depths where all is clear.
Secrets laugh, they bounce and weave,
In a world where jesters never leave.

Mysterious Currents of the Night

Moonlight dances on the sea,
Crabs are grooving, wild and free.
Fish wear hats, they all agree,
To hold a party, just for me!

Stars are laughing, flickering bright,
Seahorses twirl, what a sight!
Turtles tell jokes with all their might,
The ocean's mischief brings delight!

Serenade of the Whispering Waves

Waves are singing tunes of cheer,
Shells are clapping, lend an ear.
Gulls joke about the fish they fear,
While dolphins dance, their path is clear!

Octopus bands play on the sly,
With silly hats, oh my, oh my!
A sea breeze whispers, 'give it a try,'
As laughter echoes from nearby!

Fragments of Dreams on Sunlit Shores

On sunny sands, dreams run amok,
Kites fly high, and seashells rock.
Sandy toes and a sandman's clock,
The beach is a stage, a jester's flock!

Seagulls steal fries, what a fuss!
While kids giggle, make a plus.
With ice cream drips and a splash, a rush,
Laughter rides the waves we trust!

Love Songs in the Salty Breeze

The breeze hums sweet, a tune so bright,
Couples dance by the moon's soft light.
With lovebirds perched and hearts in flight,
A conch shell plays, it feels just right!

Sandy hearts shaped with glee,
Whispers echo, 'come dance with me.'
A clumsy crab makes his plea,
Even fish share love, can't you see?

The Heart of the Tropical Night

Crickets sing with wild guile,
A lizard dances, all in style.
Coconuts fall with a gentle thud,
While palms sway, lost in the mud.

The moon has a party, candles bright,
As stars wear their fanciest light.
A parrot laughs, but what a bore,
Could he find jokes that we adore?

The drinks are flowing, mishaps too,
I tripped on a flip-flop, oh what a view!
The tide rolls in, a soft embrace,
Making sandcastles fall from grace.

Floating dreams in coconut shells,
Mermaids giggle with their spells.
The night winds whisper tales of fun,
Where laughter sparkles, everyone runs.

A Harmony of Dusk and Dawn

As shadows dance and colors clash,
A rooster crows with quite a splash.
Tropical fruit falls from the trees,
While monkeys tease in a playful breeze.

The sun waves goodbye, all aglow,
Rabbits in tuxedos steal the show!
Pineapples in punny discussions,
While bananas make softer cushions.

Clouds turn pink with a cheeky grin,
As iguanas join the morning din.
Flip-flops flop with a funky sound,
In this paradise where joy is found.

Tides tickle toes, laughter will rule,
Nature's own circus, oh what a fool!
Lighthearted breezes sweep us away,
Creating mischief as we play.

Vibrations of a Forgotten Paradise

Old palm trees sport eccentric hats,
As seagulls conduct the choir of chats.
A hammock sways, taking a leap,
While island dreams bubble, never sleep.

Jellyfish waltz in the shallow tide,
With surfboards getting caught in their ride.
Crabs hold court, the judges so stern,
While seaweed swirls in its twisted turn.

A conch shell speaks, pretending to know,
Secrets of shells, oh, what a show!
Starfish wear socks or so they say,
Grinning wide, they dance the day.

The sun finally dips, twilight's embrace,
As the waves giggle in a playful chase.
Find your joy in this wacky view,
In an earthy party where fun is true!

Silhouettes at Dusk

The horizon blushes, an evening tease,
Lizards prance 'round, deftly with ease.
Fishermen whisper their evening plans,
While crabs hold court with their tiny fans.

Coconuts roll like boulders that dare,
While turtles trot with a casual flair.
Evening gown flowers open wide,
Waving their petals with daring pride.

The last rays of sunlight play peek-a-boo,
As shadows recite their own funny hue.
Waves tickle toes, a bubbly affair,
As fireflies dance, bursting with flair.

Oh, laughter echoes beneath the dusk,
Where playful dreams are a must.
In this quirky world of colors ablaze,
We find delight in the most fanciful ways.

Soliloquies of the Harbor Night

In the harbor where fish swim,
A bird yells, 'It's me or him!'
The moon laughs at the scene,
As sailors sip their caffeine.

A crab scuttles with great glee,
Chasing dreams beneath the sea.
A rubber duck floats by,
Quacking loud at the starry sky.

The lighthouse winks and spins,
While spooky tales begin.
The waves dance with the shore,
Who knew nights could be such a chore?

And as the night drifts on by,
The sea otters wave, oh my!
Bubbles pop like giggling sprites,
In this harbor of starry nights.

A Glimpse of Endless Blue

The ocean laughs with a roar,
While gulls squawk, wanting more.
A fish jumps high for a joke,
And lands on a sleepy bloke.

Seashells whisper to the breeze,
"Catch us if you can, oh please!"
As kids dive with a splash,
Creating mayhem in a flash.

The sun wears sunglasses blissfully,
While sandcastles stand so mischievously.
Laughter rings from every shore,
Entrancing all who dare explore.

And when the day starts to close,
Jellyfish strike a funny pose.
With a giggle and a cheer,
The endless blue brings us near.

Island Echoes in the Stillness

Whispers float on a gentle breeze,
As turtles dance, feeling at ease.
Coconuts giggle, hanging tight,
In the quiet glow of twilight.

A parrot jokes about the sun,
Saying, "Where's that shade? I'm done!"
Seashells clap as they lay,
Sharing secrets of the day.

A crab sings in a too-high key,
Causing fish to roll in glee.
The palm trees sway with a grin,
While waves play tag, wanting to win.

As night drapes its velvet cloak,
Stars laugh at the island folk.
Echoes of joy softly blend,
In stillness where fun has no end.

Veiled by the Embrace of Stars

Stars twinkle, wearing hats of light,
While owls hoot, preparing for flight.
A firefly lands on a sleepy cat,
And gives it a shout, "You're too fat!"

The night creatures come out to play,
While crickets chirp, making their way.
Moonbeams dance on the ocean's face,
As jellybeans roll in jubilant race.

Fishing boats sing with a swish,
While dolphins leap for a splashy wish.
The seaweed waves as if to say,
"Keep dancing here, come what may!"

So with stars shining high above,
This night shows just how to love.
For under this cosmic blanket, oh dear,
Laughter and joy bring us near.

Light Beyond the Jade Waters

In a land where fish wear hats,
And crabs dance in silly spats,
The sun laughs on the ocean's edge,
While seaweed sways in sea's hedge.

A dolphin lost its sense of style,
With sunglasses on, it swam a mile.
Gulls gossip about the tide,
While turtles chat, their shells their pride.

The starfish chill with ice cream scoops,
Offering flavors to passing troops.
Each wave brings a new surprise,
As laughter echoes, brightens the skies.

With coral reefs, the playground calls,
Where jellyfish play in summer brawls.
They bounce and giggle in ocean's sway,
Life's a party, come join the play!

The Allure of Starlit Retreats

Under lights that twinkle and tease,
Laughter flows with the gentle breeze.
A crab dressed in a shiny bow tie,
Declares it's time for the limbo, oh my!

The moon dips low with a cheeky grin,
As we twirl and spin, let the fun begin.
A seagull steals a potato chip,
We chase it down, not a single slip.

Bamboozled by a playful tide,
Mermaids giggle and take a ride.
With buckets of joy, we scoop and play,
The stars wink down on our merry fray.

As jellyfish join our midnight dance,
We float and drift in a sea of chance.
With every splash, we shout with glee,
In this starlit realm, forever carefree!

Notes from the Quiet Bay

In a bay where froggy frogs croak songs,
The hermit crabs wear the silliest throngs.
The anchovies swim with curious glee,
As playful otters join in the spree.

A turtle sings off-key by a tree,
While fish chuckle in perfect harmony.
Seashells gossip about a fishy tale,
Of a snail who tried to use the mail.

The waves giggle under the bright sun,
As jellybeans bounce, oh what fun!
Each splash brings laughter, a joyous sound,
In this quiet bay, where fun's always found.

The breeze winks gently, tickles the sand,
And we can't help but clap our hands.
With each wave's whisper, joy takes flight,
As we dance together in pure delight!

Murmurs of the Twilight Coast

At twilight's edge, where shadows play,
The crickets chirp a funny ballet.
A starfish mime performs on the sand,
While sea turtles join in, a funny band.

Lighthouses blink with a giggling light,
Guiding fish home, all snug and tight.
As surging waves burst into a cheer,
We laugh till dusk, our worries clear.

The sea sponge rolls in to crack a joke,
While sandcastles wobble, and then provoke.
With every giggle, the tide rolls high,
Tickling our toes, oh me, oh my!

In a world where the ocean's shy laugh flows,
We dance on the shores, where joy always grows.
With every dawn, a promise anew,
More funny moments waiting for you!

Serenade of the Sea Breeze

The seagulls squawk and dive,
Pinching fries from tourists' hands.
The waves whisper silly jokes,
While clams throw sand in the bands.

Sandy toes dance with delight,
As crabs wear hats made of seaweed.
A beach ball rolls past a kite,
While sunburned folks attempt to plead.

Surfboards crash in a fine thrash,
Mermaids giggle in the swell.
Sun-tanned friends enjoy a splash,
While jellyfish juggle as well.

As the sun sets over the bay,
A dolphin leaps in a grin.
It's all a wacky display,
Where every laugh is a win.

The Hidden Heart of Paradise

In a hut made of coconut shells,
A parrot mimics the news.
The palm trees gossip like old pals,
Sharing tales of flip-flop blues.

Tanned tourists lose their way,
Chasing shadows of a sand crab.
While local kids laugh at play,
Thinking adults are just mad.

A treasure map drawn on a napkin,
Leads to a stash of melted ice.
X marks the spot by the napkin,
Where pineapples roll, oh so nice!

As sunset paintbrushes the sky,
Laughter burbles like light rain.
With every sunset, time floats by,
We'll do it all again, insane.

Murmurs of Forgotten Beaches

Lost flip-flops line the shore,
As beach balls bounce with delight.
A coconut falls with a roar,
Hitting a hammock in flight.

Sandy kids build castles tall,
While a crab declares his throne.
Sunscreen splatters like a brawl,
As sunburnt kings make it known.

The tide brings in seaweed strands,
That tickle tourists' sun-kissed toes.
While everyone claps, "More bands!"
For the band that sings, well, who knows?

Under a pineapple tree,
Laughter echoes all around.
Every moment feels so free,
With joy, warmth, and joy abound.

Fragments of Salt and Sand

A bucket spills tons of shells,
As toddlers hunt for a prize.
Lucky finds in sandy swells,
Baking under the bright skies.

Picnic baskets burst at seams,
As ants stage their grand parade.
Kites swoop low, they swerve in dreams,
While burger flames begin to fade.

Tanning oils clash with the sun,
As laughter floats on the breeze.
Not a worry, everyone's won,
While flip-flops make silly sneeze.

Under a sky painted gold,
Even time laughs and stands still.
These memories glimmer, bold,
In the heart, they always will.

The Tides of Forgotten Dreams

The sun sets bright, it's a wild affair,
Seagulls squawking without a care.
The beach ball rolls, they chase with glee,
While sandcastles crumble, oh what a spree!

Flip-flops flying, a dog steals a snack,
Kids building towers, but where's the snack pack?
Laughter erupts, the ocean's our friend,
With sunscreen on noses, the fun will not end.

The tide dances back, playing a game,
As crabs do a jig, oh such silly fame.
Surfboards wobble, we glide and we fall,
This beach day of whimsy, let's treasure it all!

In waves of giggles, we soak up the cheer,
With friends by our side, there's nothing to fear.
The tides may roll in, but our spirits won't fade,
In turns of fun moments, sweet memories made!

Celestial Secrets Over Coral Shores

Stars twinkle down on the frothy blue,
Whispers of dolphins, do they hear us too?
With buckets and shovels, we dig down quite deep,
Finding old treasures, or just some sea creep!

The moon's a big cheese, we laugh at its sight,
Our beachside dance party goes late into night.
With ukuleles strumming a goofy old tune,
Sand slipping through fingers beneath the soft moon.

The tide tries to steal our snacks for the show,
As we dodge waves, full of giggles and glow.
A crab in a cap joins our beach jubilee,
What a funny sight, oh what glee we see!

The sea's our stage, the stars do confide,
Tales of sandy shenanigans tossed on the tide.
In this realm of laughter, we sing and we soar,
A night full of secrets forever explore!

Echoes of the Distant Waves

Waves crashing softly, they call and they tease,
Shells filled with stories, a crasher in the breeze.
With laughter as loud as a seagull's bold cry,
The sand holds our secrets and dreams that won't die.

A bucket of sand, with hiccuping glee,
We sing to the ocean, oh can't you see?
The tide rolls in fast, wearing a big grin,
As we tumble and rumble, let the fun begin!

Frothy waves splash, a giggle parade,
While fish in the sea just roll their eyes, played!
We build silly monsters, our castle ascent,
A fortress of joy, why's the tide so bent?

With beach balls and umbrellas all out of line,
We sketch in the sand, our goofiest design.
Echoes of laughter, sweet songs of delight,
In a dance with the waves, we're stars of the night!

The Heartbeat of Hidden Shores

At dawn's early light, the surf starts to hum,
Watch out, here come the marshmallow bum!
Flip-flops encounter a crab with a grin,
Chasing the waves as they wince and spin.

Sandy shenanigans lead to a splash,
In our quest for treasures, we move with a dash.
The jellyfish giggles as we run by fast,
Dashing through troubles, our worries won't last!

Picnics of snacks, oh what a delight,
Too much jelly, a sticky old sight!
Seashells are gathering tales of our fun,
As we wave back to the ocean, our own number one.

With laughter and bubbles, the heart beats anew,
The shores of our stories, forever in view.
In a whirl of beach games, we dance 'round the day,
Every moment together, hip-hip-hooray!

The Solitude of Whispered Breezes

The wind told secrets, soft and sly,
It teased my hat and made it fly.
A tree giggled when I passed by,
I waved it back, oh, don't be shy!

Clouds rolled like laughter in the air,
I chased one down without a care.
It turned and played hide-and-seek,
With sunshine's rays, quite cheek to cheek.

A squirrel joined me on the quest,
With acorn snacks, we were the best!
Together we plotted a grand scheme,
To catch the breeze—a silly dream!

So off we went, our giggles gleamed,
In a world where nothing seemed,
To matter much but fun and play,
We danced with whispers through the day.

Dreams Cast by Starry Nights

Stars twinkled like winking bugs,
I laid on grass, feeling all snug.
The moon wore shades, looked quite cool,
While frogs held court in the moonlit pool.

The milky way danced with silly glee,
A cosmic ballet, oh what a spree!
Aliens giggled, played tag with beams,
While I tried to count all my dreams.

A comet zoomed by, said, "Catch my tail!"
I threw a wish, oh please don't fail!
But it just laughed and sped away,
To find another starry play.

So I drifted off, full of delight,
With dreams of capers till morning light.
And when I woke, I felt so spry,
Still dancing under that twinkling sky.

The Lure of Ceaseless Mysteries

A treasure map made of jello slice,
Led me to giggles, more than once or thrice.
X marked the spot, but it turned out to be,
A picnic with ants who begged for tea.

Waves chatted secrets to the shore,
As crabs performed a tap dancing score.
I tried to join, but slipped on sand,
Only to find a jellyfish band.

The stars above whispered back and forth,
"Who would have thought of this quirk's worth?"
I laughed so much, my cheeks turned bright,
Joining the creatures in the starlit night.

In the end, the mysteries were clear,
That laughter and fun are always near.
For every challenge or puzzle in tow,
Find the joke, let joy freely flow.

Navigation of the Cosmic Waters

With a rubber duck, I sailed the space,
Through cosmic waters, I found my place.
Stars were my crew, with a wink and a grin,
Colorful fish danced, let the fun begin!

Galaxies spun like cotton candy,
I tried to catch one, it felt so dandy.
Each twinkling splash was a giggle and cheer,
In this vast ocean, there was nothing to fear.

A whale blew bubbles, shaped like pies,
While octopuses played with sticky ties.
I joined their game, a vast cosmic tease,
Weathered the waves with the greatest of ease.

As I navigated through laughter's tide,
With my trusty duck as captain and guide.
I found that adventure, no matter how far,
Always sails best with a joyful star.

Echoes of Legends in the Breeze

The parrot sings tales of old,
While crabs dance in the sand so bold.
Laughter floats on salty air,
Mermaids giggle, but do they care?

The coconut falls with a clunk,
Islanders think it's pure junk.
But gather 'round for stories grand,
Of treasure buried deep in sand!

A turtle races, oh so slow,
While fish take bets on the show.
The waves keep whispering their tune,
As seagulls argue with the moon.

With every gust, a joke is spun,
Unearthed laughter, pure island fun!
So raise a drink, let joy grow wide,
In the ocean's silly tide.

The Gentle Hand of Time on Paradise

Time tickles palms like playful breeze,
Swaying between bright coconuts trees.
The sun slips slowly, wearing its hat,
While crabs hold council, quite round and flat.

The clock is a hammock, swaying with glee,
Forget the minutes, drink coconut tea!
Sandy footprints lead joyfully,
As dolphins grin at what they see.

The gentle waves, they shuffle and slide,
Urging us to join the ride.
With every tick, a joke unfurls,
As laughter rolls in, swirls and twirls.

So let the hours do their dance,
Life's a party, let's take a chance!
Under the stars, merriment flows,
With breezy tales that everyone knows.

Traces of Stars on Wavy Waters

Stars flip-flop on the rolling tide,
Wiggling like fish on a summer ride.
The moon dons shades, looking quite cool,
As dolphins splash, they break the rule.

The sea laughs loudly, tickling the night,
As jellyfish glow, a whimsical sight.
In this dance where joys collide,
The waves invite all to join the ride.

An octopus sneezes, causing a stir,
While seagulls attempt to dance but prefer a slur.
All the fish join the cosmic dance,
Stars above giggle at their chance.

Under the shimmer, secrets abound,
As laughter echoes, bond is found.
With every splash, another jest,
In the water's heart, we find our zest.

Sunrise over Ghostly Shores

Ghosts of sandcastles, once proud and tall,
Now play with shadows, do they recall?
The sun rises up, providing a show,
As sleepy seashells wink to and fro.

The breeze whispers secrets, a mischievous tease,
Stirring up laughter with effortless ease.
As sunrise paints skies in shades of delight,
Even the ghosts can't resist the bright light.

Waves crash gently, like snores of the night,
While crabs join in, hopping left, then right.
Mirth erupts like foam on the crest,
Amongst these shores, who knows what's best?

With each dawn, hilarity wakes,
As sun-drenched mischief the shoreline shakes.
The laughter of spirits fills the air,
In reignited joy, we all share.

The Pulse of the Coral Lagoon

Fish wear suits, they swim in style,
Crabs hold meetings with a wacky smile.
Sea turtles gossip, tales they weave,
Underwater parties, you won't believe!

Jellyfish dance like they're on a spree,
With disco lights, so wild and free.
The clownfish crack jokes, a real delight,
While octopuses juggle, what a sight!

Seashells gossip by the sandy dunes,
While starfish strut to their own tunes.
The waves applaud, oh what a show,
In the coral lagoon, laughter will flow!

A dolphin dives with a playful flip,
Anemones smile, they don't even trip.
Underwater giggles fill the air,
Joy is abundant, everywhere!

Canvas of the Setting Sun

The sun paints colors, a brush in the sky,
While seagulls squabble, oh my, oh my!
Pirate parrots squawk with glee,
Stealing snacks from a careless bee!

Sandy toes wiggle, dancing around,
As shells gossip, the funniest sound.
The horizon swells, a curious plot,
Where mermaids plot mischief — oh what a lot!

Crabs in tuxedos, looking so grand,
Hold a soirée on the warm, soft sand.
Starfish serve drinks, oh what a treat,
While kids chase waves, skipping on feet!

Sunset's laughter, in colors bright,
As twilight sneaks in, painting the night.
The best magic show, for all to behold,
The canvas of sun sets, a sight to unfold!

Solace in the Island Breeze

The palm trees giggle, swaying in line,
As the coconut clowns play fetch with sunshine.
Kids chase rainbows that flutter near,
While ice cream drips and laughter's clear!

Tropical birds dress up for a ball,
With feathers so bright, they dazzle us all.
Lizards wearing hats, oh what a tease,
Basking in warmth, enjoying the breeze!

Waves send whispers of silly tales,
Of underwater pranks and gusty gales.
The sunset nods, giving a wink,
As night emerges, it's time to drink!

Fireflies dance like a twinkling show,
While laughter erupts in a playful flow.
The island hums with a cheerful tease,
In the solace found, oh what a breeze!

Horizon's Edge of Mystery

Where the sea meets the sky, funny things happen,
Like dolphins in suits, who love to start clappin'.
The horizon leans close, curious to peek,
At the jellyfish jokes that make the waves squeak!

Clouds drift by, sharing silly dreams,
Of mermaids who twirl in sparkly streams.
With seashells chuckling, they all conspire,
To tease the sun until it's on fire!

The sand becomes canvas, where footprints play,
With silly shapes that giggle all day.
Seagulls make faces, wise and absurd,
While fish write poems, their voices unheard!

At dusk, the horizon whispers a jest,
A riddle perhaps, can you guess the best?
In this land of mystery, fun never fades,
Where laughter is painted in bright periwades!

The Lure of Twilight Waters

The fish wear tiny hats, I swear,
They hold a dance with quite the flair,
Twirling beneath the stars' bright lights,
As crabs play drums on sandy nights.

The mermaids gossip, tails all a-twirl,
Sharing secrets in a whirling whirl,
While sea turtles race in a slow crawl,
And seagulls laugh at it all—what a ball!

The waves hum tunes to sleepy stars,
Jellyfish twinkle like tiny cars,
We'd join in, but we've lost our shoes,
Splashing in laughter, what could we lose?

So, come for a swim, don't take a nap,
Let's catch the sunset in a fishy trap,
With all this fun, how can one stay dry?
We'll be pristine until the sun's goodbye!

Enchanted by Island Mist

The fog waltzes in with a playful grin,
Hiding coconuts like cheeky kin,
Parrots giggle, rustling the trees,
While monkeys swing, aiming to please.

Drifting on air, the mist is a tease,
Catching the birds that come with the breeze,
It tickles our noses, makes us sneeze loud,
While we dance together, lost in the crowd.

A crab in a tux struts across the sand,
His dance so fine, isn't it grand?
The fish wear sunglasses and throw a bash,
The party's a blast, let's make a splash!

So, lose your worries, let's take a chance,
Join the rhythm of an island dance,
Wrapped in mist, let laughter unroll,
What's life without fun? It feeds the soul!

Reflections on a Velvet Wave

A wave races in, all silky and sly,
It tickles my toes—oh my, oh my!
With splashes of laughter under the moon,
The ocean sings us a bubbly tune.

Starlit echoes bounce off the shore,
As fish throw a party, and who could ignore?
They wear little crowns, call each other king,
While shells cheer loudly, "Let's dance and sing!"

The rhythm of waves, like a swaying drum,
Makes everyone dance, even the glum.
A crab on a skateboard, what a sight,
Rolling past us, giggling with delight.

So let's ride the curls of this oceanic fun,
With laughter as bright as the morning sun,
For moments like these, oh so surreal,
Make the waves dance, that's the biggest deal!

Imaginations in the Tropical Twilight

As twilight creeps with a silly face,
We build castles of sand in this playful place,
Seashells whisper secrets, or so they claim,
While we craft stories in this whimsical game.

An octopus juggles, it's quite a sight,
While starfish cheer with all of their might,
The tide rolls in with a playful wave,
And everyone here feels fancy and brave.

Bananas in pajamas float on by,
Joined by turtles who soar and fly,
Underneath palms that sway like a band,
We sing ocean ballads, all unplanned.

So grab your friends, let's be a bit wild,
Join in the fun, let laughter be styled,
For as the sun dips down from the sky,
We'll dance under stars, waving worries goodbye!

Twilight Tales of a Hidden Cove

In a cove where crabs wear hats,
And fish gossip like old chitchat,
The seaweed dances with the tide,
While turtles giggle, wide-eyed.

A clam sings opera, oh so grand,
As starfish cheer and take a stand.
The moonlight bathes the scene just right,
Where laughter echoes through the night.

But oh, the seagulls steal the show,
With prankish antics, row by row.
They swoop and dive, a feathery fleet,
While dolphins dive with flippant feet.

So sip your coconut with glee,
Join in the laughter, wild and free.
The hidden cove, a comical sight,
Where twilight tales bring pure delight.

Ocean's Cradle at Dusk.

As the sun dips low, the waves all cheer,
A clam in shades sips salty beer.
Fish play poker in a coral nook,
While squids publish their own funny book.

In the cradle of waves so soft,
A jellyfish dances, swaying aloft.
Octopuses juggle with flair and grace,
As barnacles chuckle at slow-paced race.

The sailboats wave like they know a joke,
While flip-flops fly from a silly bloke.
The ocean's cradle rocks with laughter,
As sea life plays, chasing ever after.

So as dusk settles and stars appear,
Join the hullabaloo, shed your fear.
For in this cradle, pure cheer will reign,
In a world where humor's the main domain.

Whispers of the Seabreeze

The seabreeze carries soft-spoken pranks,
As pelicans dance on slippery planks.
Whispers of waves tickle the shore,
While fish toss jokes and ask for more.

A crab plays tag with a sneaky shoe,
While dolphins splash, making hullabaloo.
The whispering breeze sings gentle tunes,
As clowns in the ocean wear funny balloons.

Yet, look close at the hermit's new shell,
It's the cookie jar where secrets dwell.
Surprise awaits with every gust,
As laughter bubbles, a joyful must.

So breathe in deep the salty air,
Join the whispers, the jokes to share.
In this seaside kingdom full of jest,
The seabreeze brings mirth and a spirit of fest.

Shadows Beneath the Palm Trees

In the shadows, where the coconuts sway,
A monkey grins, ready to play.
With a wink and a twist, he swings with glee,
While palm fronds flutter, inviting the spree.

Lizards wear glasses, reading the news,
While crabs kick back in snazzy shoes.
The shadows grow long, laughter erupt,
As goofy sea turtles tumble and sup.

Beneath the palms, the parties ignite,
With glow-in-the-dark fish lighting the night.
Their jokes ripple out like waves in the sea,
Creating a symphony of humor and glee.

So join the fun in the moonlit arc,
Where shadows bring laughter, igniting a spark.
In this palm tree realm of laughs and fun,
Every dusk promises jokes just begun.

Stars Drifting Over Turquoise Waters

On a boat made of laughter and dreams,
Fish wear sunglasses, or so it seems.
Jellyfish dancing to the sea's great song,
They invite all the turtles to come sing along.

Crabs in a conga line under a moonbeam,
They've got moves that'll make you want to scream!
Seagulls are gossiping up in the breeze,
Trading old tales, as they feast on some cheese.

The waves laugh loud, tickling the shore,
They play hide-and-seek with flip-flops galore.
Stars are winking, adding to the jest,
Who knew the ocean could throw such a fest?

And as the night drapes its shimmering gown,
I spot a mermaid who's lost her crown.
With a splash and a giggle, she takes a bow,
The ocean's a party; come join us now!

The Poetry of the Quiet Coastline

The quiet coast whispers secrets at night,
Where seaweed sings softly, all feels just right.
Shells tell their stories, each one unique,
While crabs practice yoga, it's quite the peak.

A lighthouse winks as if telling a joke,
While fishermen dream on their floating cloak.
Tides play charades with the gulls overhead,
While sandcastles mourn that their builders have fled.

Dolphins giggle, leaping with flair,
Taking windsurfing lessons, oblivious to care.
In the distance, a clam shimmies in glee,
As he rolls in the surf to the rhythm of three.

Just a glance at the ocean, and you'll find,
That silliness flourishes in waves—purely divine.
In the realm of the surf, with the sun dipping low,
Life's perfect distraction is just letting go.

Embracing the Twilight Tide

The sunset giggles with orange and pink,
Mermaids take selfies and sip from the sink.
Oysters are rapping, while dolphins beatbox,
As starfish thumb-wrestle on their sandy blocks.

The sky blushes bright, a playful charade,
While the tide rolls in with a wave serenade.
Octopuses juggle, while crabs eat popcorn,
Oh, what a sight 'til the break of dawn!

Turtles paint rainbows with brushes so wide,
As they dive in the sea for a fun water slide.
With a flip and a splash, they make quite a scene,
In this wacky wave wonderland, all feels like a dream.

As stars start to twinkle, the fun's not done,
For the sea holds secrets of laughter and run.
The night calls us forth, with a chuckle so bright,
In the arms of the tide, our spirits take flight!

Beneath the Sugarloaf Skies

Where cotton candy clouds drift and swirl,
Pineapple drinks make the sea breeze twirl.
Fish pull pranks on the passing boats,
While turtles tune up their sweet vocal notes.

Balloons float by with a giggle or two,
As jellybeans twinkle in waters so blue.
Seagulls host tea parties with delicate grace,
While otters make ruckus at a slow-motion race.

The sunset's a circus, a color parade,
Even the seaweed has joined in the trade.
With bubbles and laughter escaping each wave,
We find joy in nature, oh how it behaves!

As night brushes softly with stars that align,
The ocean sings sweet nothings, divine.
In this joyful embrace of the twilight glow,
The magic of laughter is ours to bestow.

The Call of the Gentle Surf

Waves tickle toes in playful jest,
Shells chuckle loud, they know best.
Seagulls squawk with feathered flair,
While crabs dance like they haven't a care.

Sun hats fly, a breeze the thief,
Dune buggies zoom, startling the reef.
Beach umbrellas tip in glee,
As sunscreen battles an army of sand, oh me!

Laughter spills like water bright,
Flip-flops caught in the twilight's light.
Even fish are laughing too,
As they sneak up on unsuspecting shoe.

With giggles echoing far and wide,
A day at sea is a sweetened ride.
So come, dear friend, join the fun,
Under the sun, the laughter's begun.

Shimmering Shadows at Sundown

Coconuts sway with a cheeky grin,
As shadows stretch, the fun begins.
The sunset blushes, oh what a sight,
While crickets start their evening light.

Flip-flops squeak a silly song,
As beachgoers dance, and silliness throngs.
Tiki torches flicker, casting odd shapes,
While everyone swaps funny landscape grapes.

With every splash, a laugh erupts,
From sandcastle kings, hilarious pups.
Even the stars are up for the game,
As jellyfish glow, calling out names.

So toast to the dusk, with coconut cheer,
With funny tales of the day, oh dear!
Let shadows twirl in the warm, bright glow,
For beneath this sunset, laughter will flow.

Constellations Over Eternal Sands

The stars gossip in a twinkling spree,
While sand crabs plot their destiny.
Moonbeams laugh, casting silly sights,
As galaxies crack jokes all night.

Tired turtles stretch in slow-motion dance,
Finding their groove in a starry trance.
Shooting stars dart, a raucous flight,
As people ponder, 'Is that a fish or a kite?'

With every grunt from the ocean bed,
The salty breeze whispers giggles instead.
Distant islands chuckle, keeping score,
While mermaids roll their eyes at the shore.

As laughter mingles with the ocean's sigh,
We raise our voices, and together we cry.
In this cosmic jest of the night sky,
Let's keep the laughter, oh me, oh my!

The Breath of the Coral Reefs

Tickling fish in a swirling dance,
Coral castles give a playful glance.
Octopuses giggle through their masks,
While seaweed waves as it happily basks.

Bubble-blowers have a bubbly dream,
In the underwater world, the bubbles beam.
Anemones laugh, their colors provide,
As clownfish swim with a comical pride.

With every ripple, a chuckle flows,
Seashells hide treasures, and secrets they know.
So dive on in, the water's all right,
Where laughter and bubbles are quite the sight.

In coral gardens where silliness reigns,
The ocean's heart beats with joy and gains.
Join the dance, feel the flippered glee,
For in every wave, there's a giggle, you see!

Journeys through a Tropical Whisper

A crab danced with a nearby shoe,
While parrots squawked a tune or two.
The palm tree hat was quite the sight,
But it fell when the wind took flight.

A turtle tried to ride a wave,
But soon discovered it was brave.
With laughter bubbling in the sea,
It slid back home quite happily.

The fish held a conch shell parade,
While snorkelers thought it was handmade.
A dolphin photobombed the scene,
With antics that made the crowd beam.

So here beneath the shade's embrace,
We giggled at each creature's grace.
For fun awaits in every nook,
In each tide pool and cranny's crook.

A Tapestry of Sun-kissed Dreams

A sunburned tourist sought the bar,
But ended up with a coconut star.
It blinked and winked, what a surprise,
While taking selfies with the flies!

Beach towels tangled in a mess,
A picnic turned into a press.
With sand in sandwiches galore,
Who knew lunch could be such a chore?

Seagulls argued over a chip,
While one attempted a daring flip.
The waves cheered on their feathery foes,
As laughter mixed with ocean blows.

And when the sun began to sink,
We gathered 'round for one last drink.
With jokes and jests, our hearts did gleam,
In this land of zany, sun-kissed dreams.

Harmonies of the Secret Bay

Banana boats zoomed with glee,
While frogs croaked in perfect harmony.
A parrot stole a snack or two,
Juicy mango? Yes, that'll do!

The hermit crabs held a race,
Though all were quite the slowpoke case.
Their shells adorned with glitter bright,
As spectators cheered with delight.

A fisherman hummed a silly tune,
While searching for jigs and spoons.
His catch was a boot, oh what a shame,
He proudly claimed it was the aim!

As twilight whispered to the sea,
We laughed 'til dawn, so wild and free.
For every moment here was gay,
In the melodies of the secret bay.

Rhythms of the Forgotten Isle

A monkey on a skateboard flew,
Chasing coconuts that rolled askew.
With giggles echoing through the trees,
While crabs hosted their karaoke spree!

An iguana posed for a pic,
Unbothered by the camera's click.
With shades and a hat, quite stylish too,
It claimed the beach as its own venue.

Pineapples tumbled down the hill,
While everyone laughed, trying for a thrill.
A coconut fell, and what a roar!
As heads turned to see, "Who's on the floor?"

In dance we twirled; oh what a sight,
As rhythms filled the fading night.
In every twinkle, laughter flowed,
Among the beats of the isle's abode.

Melodies of a Coastal Mirage

Seagulls squawk with silly glee,
While crabs dance on the sandy spree.
Waves giggle as they race ashore,
Telling secrets lost in ocean's lore.

A beach ball bounces, laughter flies,
Dancers slip as seagulls size.
With popsicles melting in the sun,
A race for ice cream, all in fun!

Sun hats wobble, kite tails sway,
Wind's a prankster in bright array.
Catch that frisbee, oh what a feat,
It lands in your soda, how sweet!

When twilight whispers, the fun won't end,
Glow sticks shimmer, and night we'll send.
With starry winks and crabs that stroll,
Tonight's a laughter, that's our goal!

The Lighthouses of Lost Stories

A lighthouse winks on tipsy rocks,
Its keeper wears mismatched socks.
With tales of pirates and fish so tall,
The seagulls giggle, they know it all.

One bulb shines bright, the other dims,
As locals craft some sea shanty hymns.
Whispers of mermaids and treasure maps,
Every tale grows with cheeky chaps.

Sandy footprints lead to nowhere,
Where narrow-minded crabs start their dare.
Spectacles held up by fragile pride,
While jellyfish join the joyride.

When the moon's a crank, and stars get loud,
Flickering lights dance with the crowd.
In this lighthouse of stories galore,
We find the magic, and laugh even more!

Bastions of Castle Rocks

On craggy cliffs, a castle stands,
With guards made out of seaweed bands.
A dragon snores, dreaming of pie,
While fish in armor march on by.

Lost in reverie, the knights play chess,
With crabby threats, they can't digress.
Riding tides on plastic steeds,
Off to fetch their salty beads.

A prince gets tangled in seaweed's clutch,
His castle helm caused way too much.
With laughter echoing through the night,
They stage a duel, all in delight.

When dawn arrives, the jesters grin,
For every castle holds room for sin.
In laughter's light and a splash of cheer,
These bastions, oh so dear!

Patches of Heaven in Aquamarine

Under skies of vivid hue,
Turtles ride on waves of blue.
They wear sunglasses, looking so cool,
While dolphins dance in shimmering pool.

Picnic blankets under palm trees sway,
As frogs challenge their hops today.
In sun hats flipped, the laughter stacks,
While snacks fly high on joyful tracks.

A beachcomber slips on wet sand,
Seashells tumble as giggles expand.
With juice boxes spilled, all in good cheer,
Their smiles sparkle like the sea dear.

As the sun sets, they share a pie,
And count the stars that light the sky.
In patches of heaven, oh what a scene,
Life is funny, and so serene!

Dance of the Moon on Silvery Waves

The moon spins round like a disco ball,
Fish join in, giving it their all.
Starfish tap dance on the coral stage,
While crabs moonwalk, full of rage.

Jellyfish float with their fancy flair,
Chasing seafoam without a care.
Octopus grooves, limbs in a twist,
All in a whirl, how could we resist?

Seahorses shimmy, so slick and spry,
While turtles stop to laugh and sigh.
Underwater parties never cease,
As bubbles burst, bringing us peace.

The night is alive, a sparkling sight,
Under moonlight, everything feels right.
In this watery world, joy flows and sways,
A rhythmic delight, the ocean plays.

Chasing Shadows Between the Tides

A crab got lost in the swirling sand,
Chasing his shadow, thought he was grand.
Waves rolled in with a chuckle so deep,
'You can't catch what's yours, back to sleep!'

Seagulls swoop low with a cheer and a squawk,
Cracking jokes as they strut on the rock.
No need to worry, they said with a laugh,
'Just don't ask the fish for their photograph!'

With a splash of humor and a wink from the tide,
Even the barnacles join in for the ride.
Laughter echoes down to the clams in their beds,
'What's so funny? Wish we had legs instead!'

The shadows play tag as the sun says goodnight,
Making silly shapes in the soft moonlight.
From laughter to giggles, they twist and they glide,
Chasing each other, they dance with great pride.

When Waves Kiss the Sandy Embrace

Sandy toes giggle as waves rush ashore,
Salty kisses leaving us wanting more.
A flip-flop flops off, it starts to protest,
'Oh no! Not the water, I'm not ready yet!'

Seashells laugh, all polished and bright,
Shells cracking jokes, what a silly sight!
A crab says, 'Why do we scramble on sand?'
To catch quick snacks that are getting out hand!'

Waves gather round for a quirky parade,
Spraying all beachgoers, who laugh and get laid.
Umbrellas dance as a wind makes them twirl,
While sandcastles wobble, waiting to hurl!

As twilight settles, the humor survives,
Under the stars, where every joy thrives.
With laughter in hearts and sand in our hair,
We dance with the waves, without a care.

Stories Carried by the Ocean Mist

The ocean whispers secrets in a breezy tone,
While dolphins giggle, playing on their own.
'What did the sea say to the boat?' asks one,
'You're all afloat, but I'm having more fun!'

As mist rolls in, it tells stories untold,
Of pirates and treasures, glittering gold.
But seagulls mock loudly and won't let it slide,
'All those tall tales need a better guide!'

Crabs hold a conference on the damp land,
Arguing over who's the best in the band.
They strum on their shells, a crustacean tune,
While the waves just laugh, 'We're all here for the moon!'

So if you ever wander with eyes on the sea,
Remember the tales of humor and glee.
With laughter in currents and jokes in each mist,
The ocean's a stage, none shall be missed!

www.ingramcontent.com/pod-product-compliance
Lightning Source LLC
Chambersburg PA
CBHW072222070526
44585CB00015B/1449